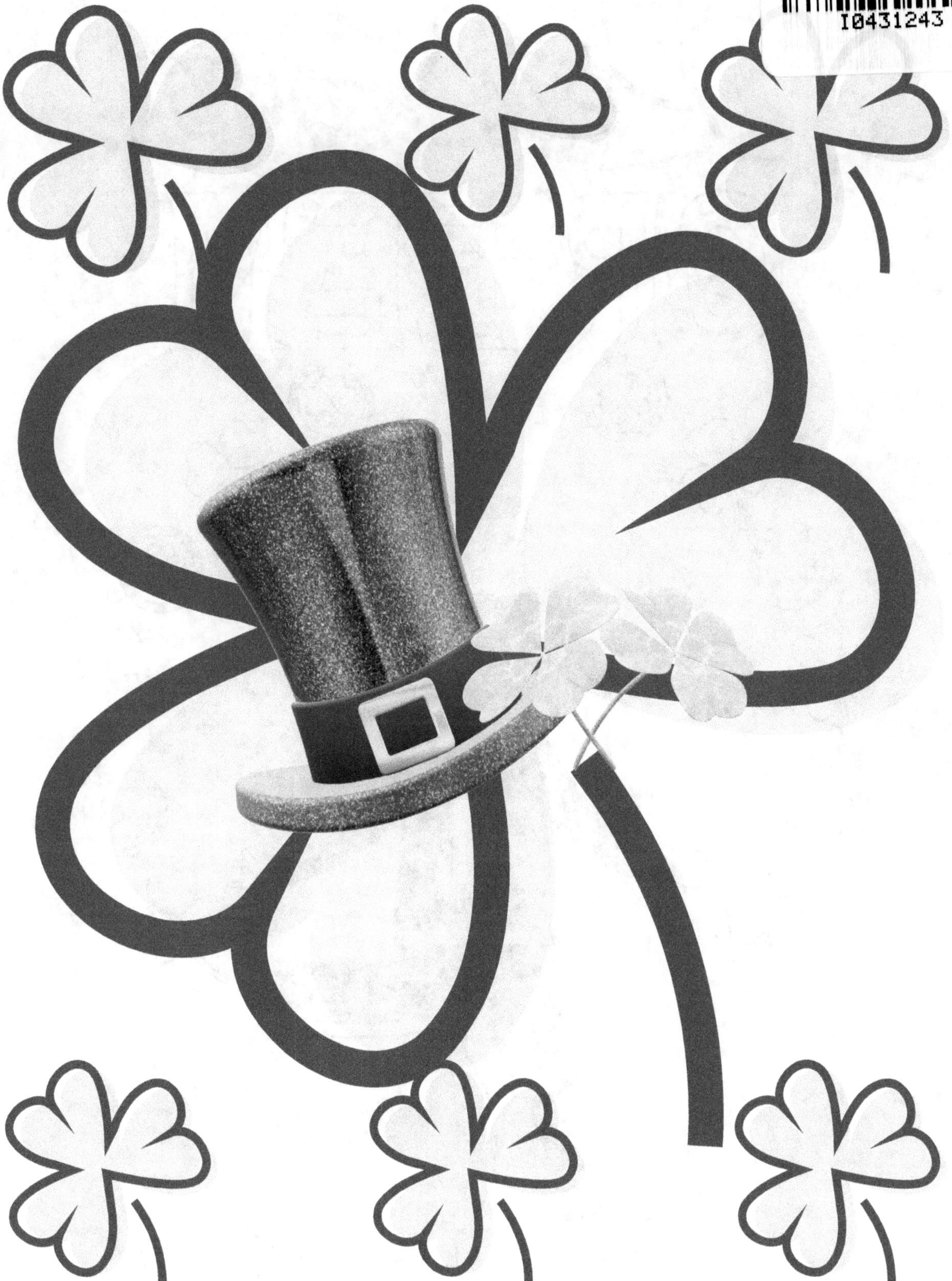

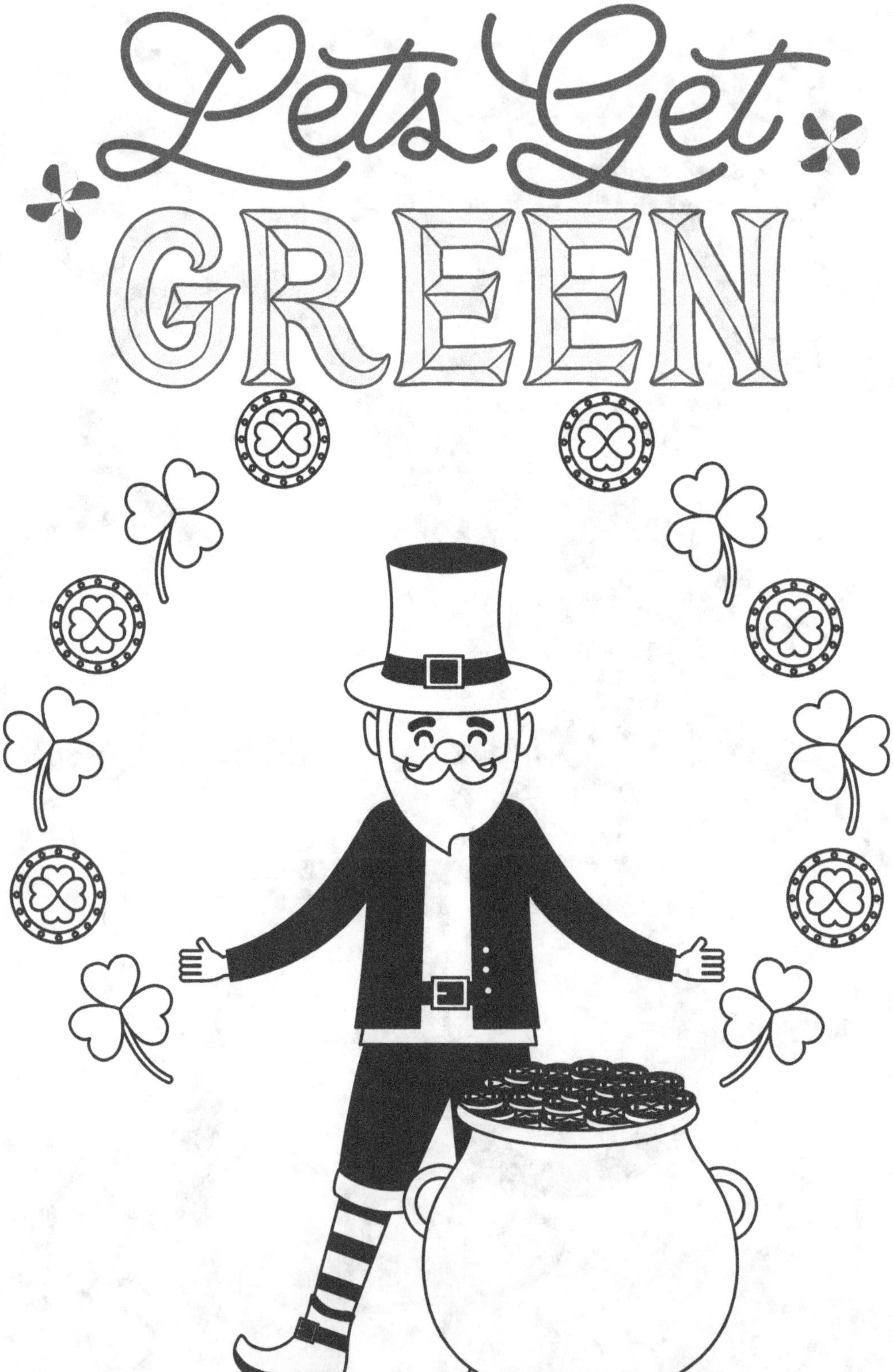
Lets Get
GREEN

St. Patrick's Day
Love

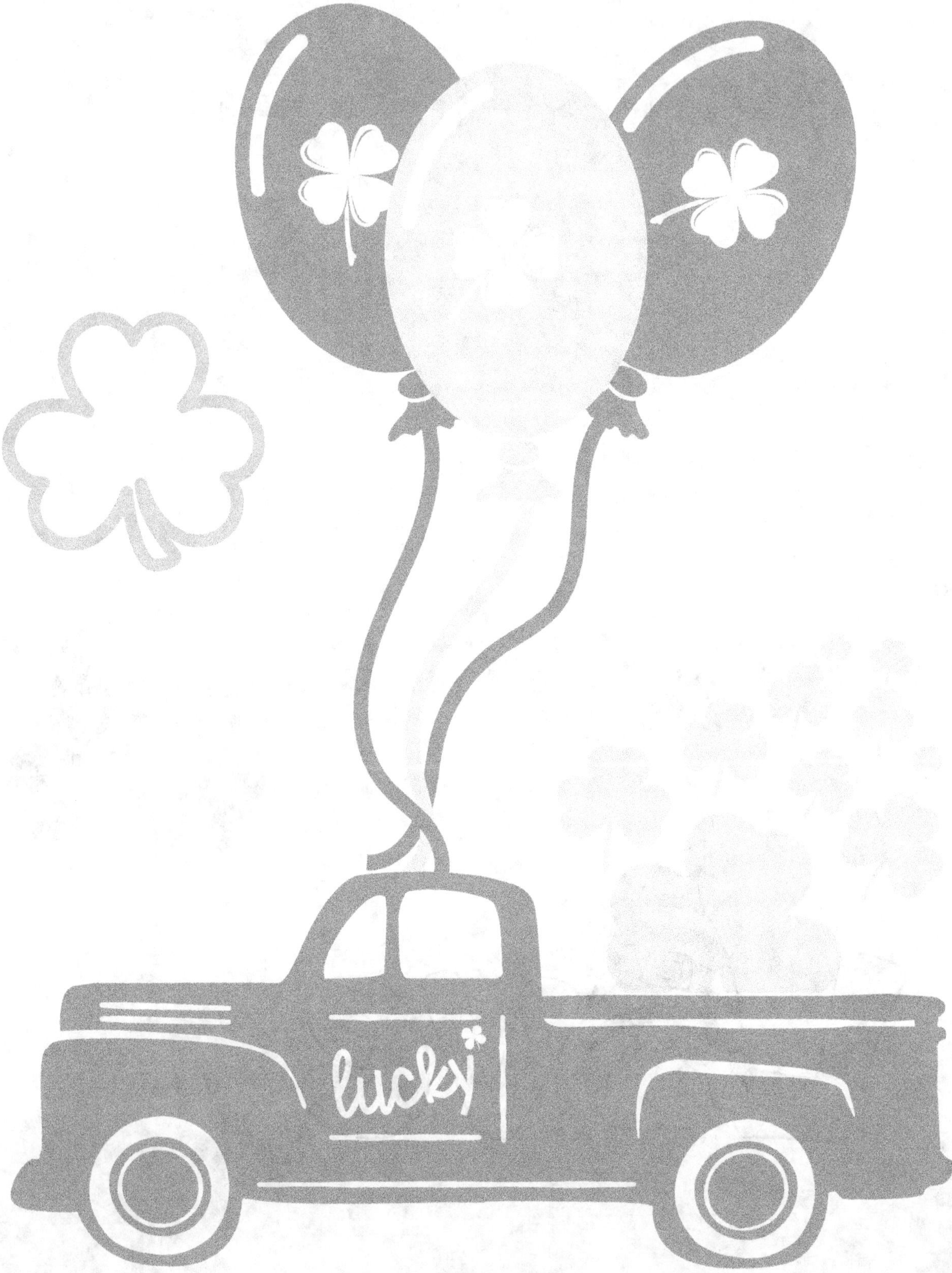
lucky

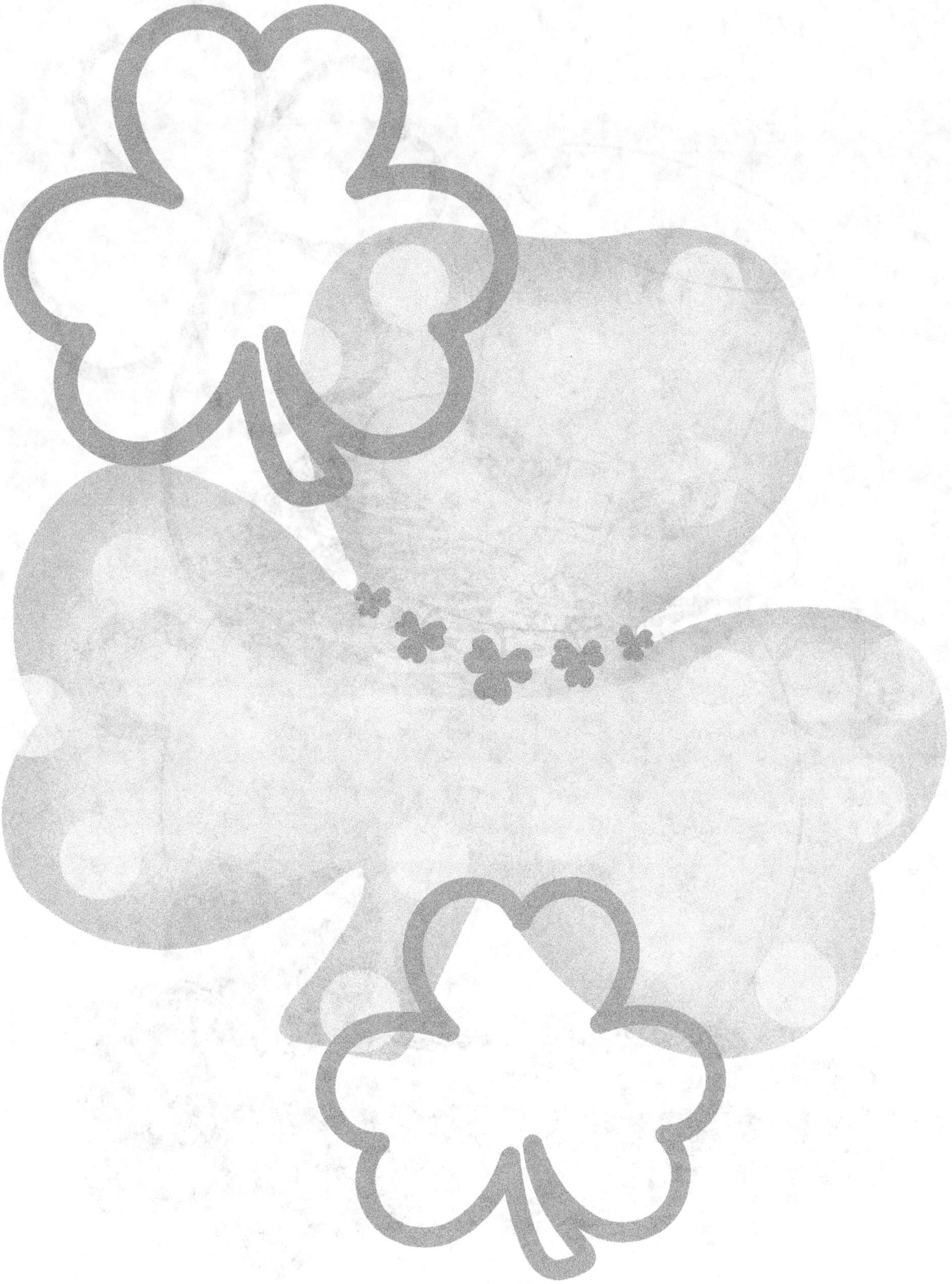

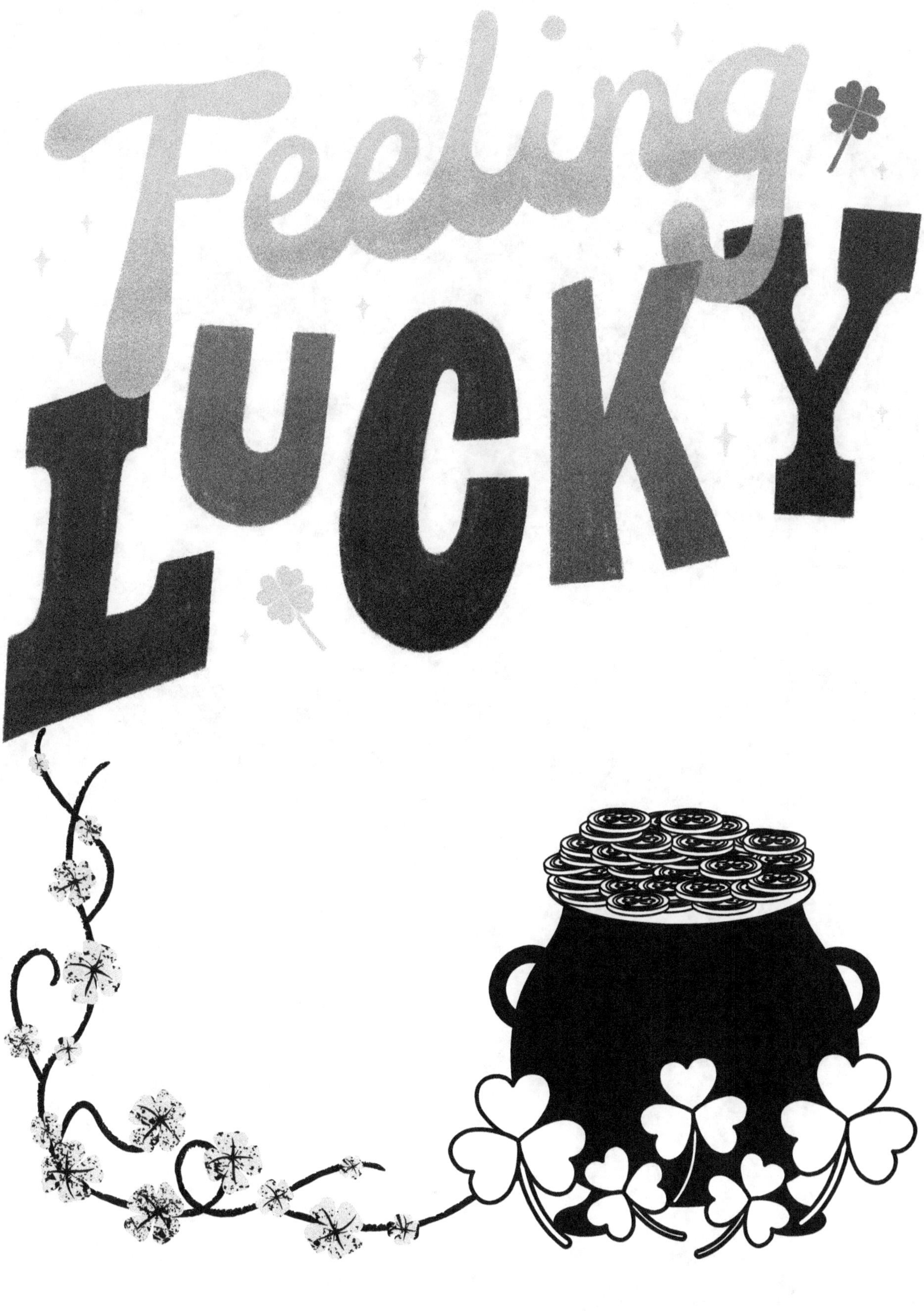
Feeling
LUCKY

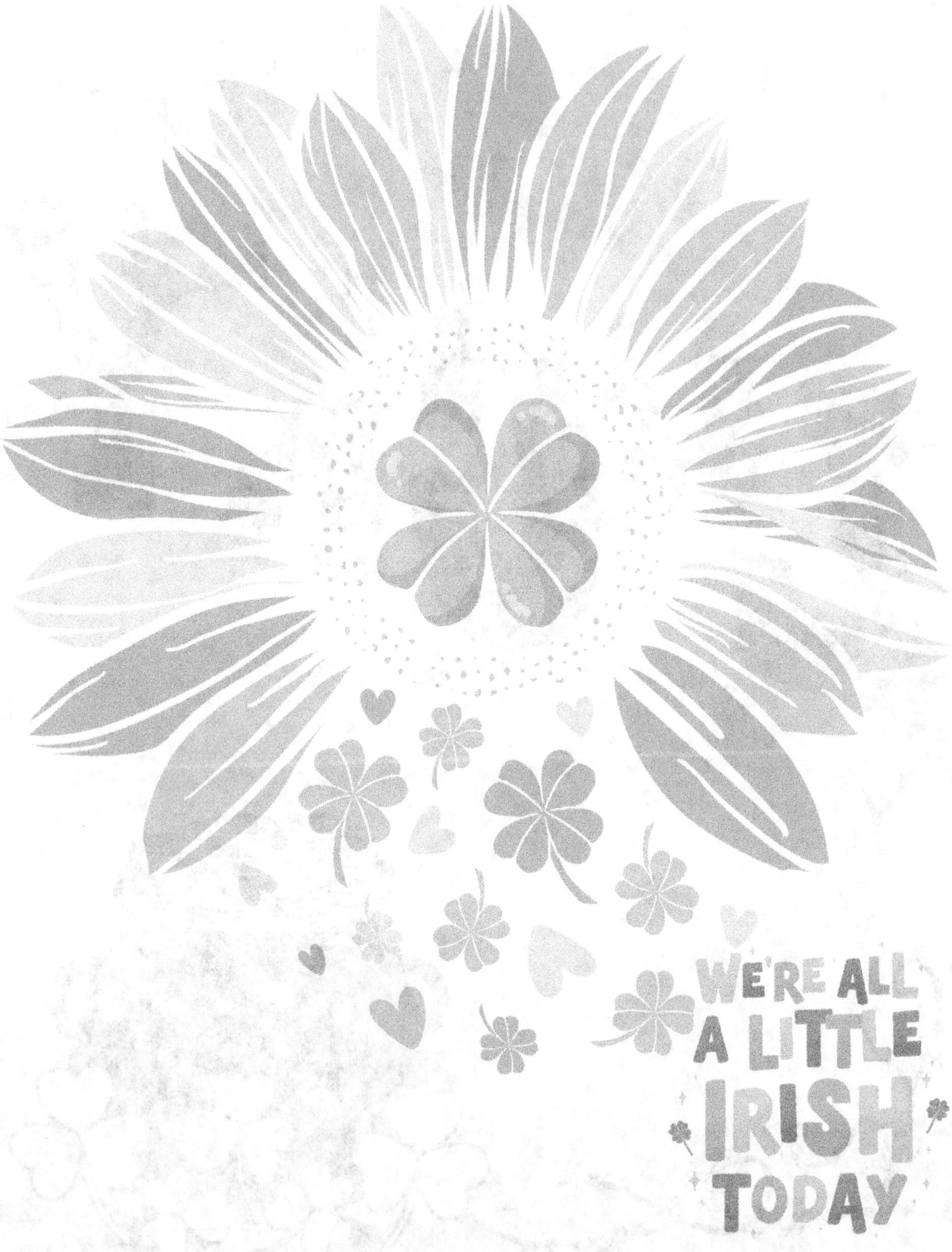
WE'RE ALL
A LITTLE
IRISH
TODAY

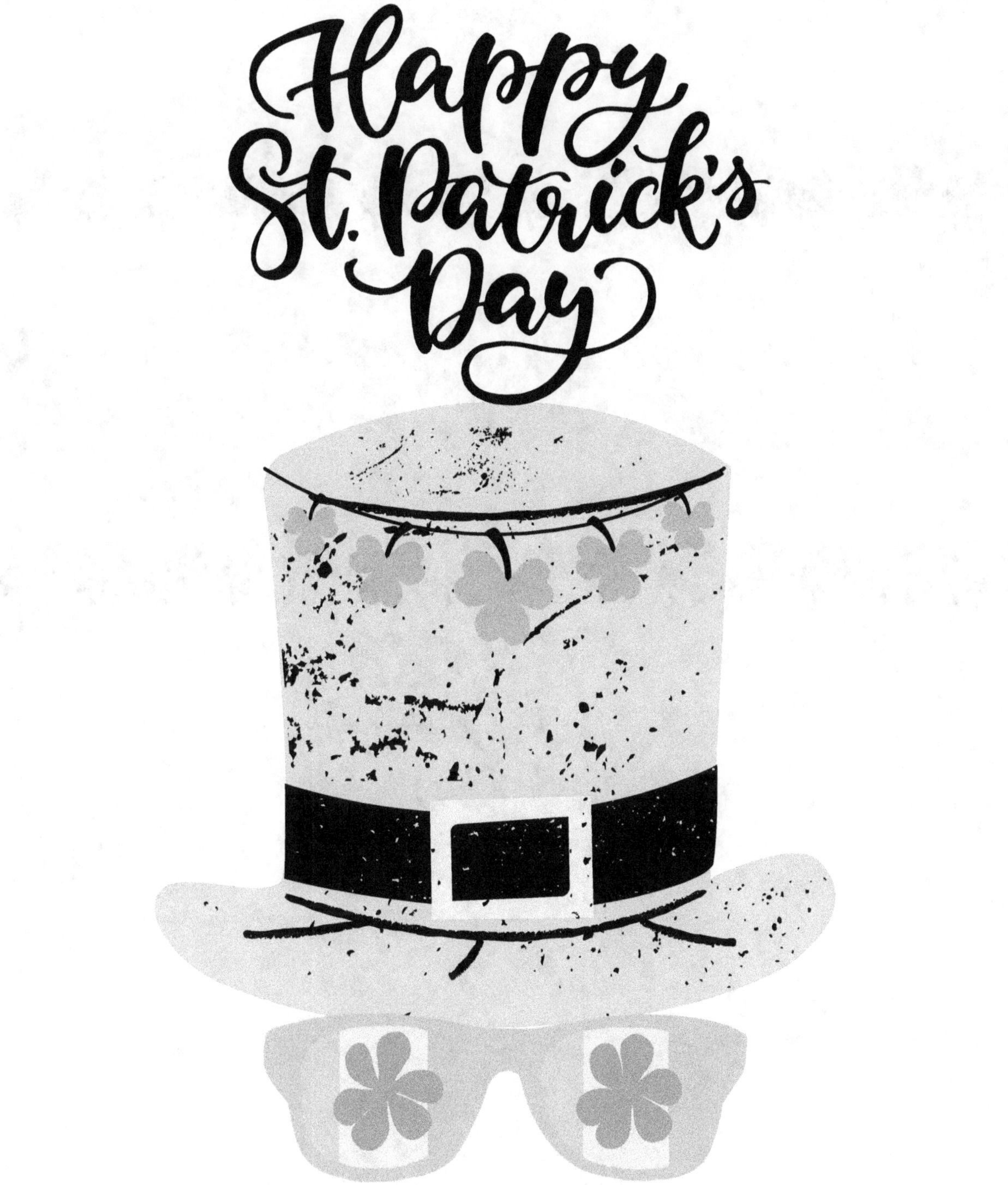
Happy
St. Patrick's
Day

CELEBRATE

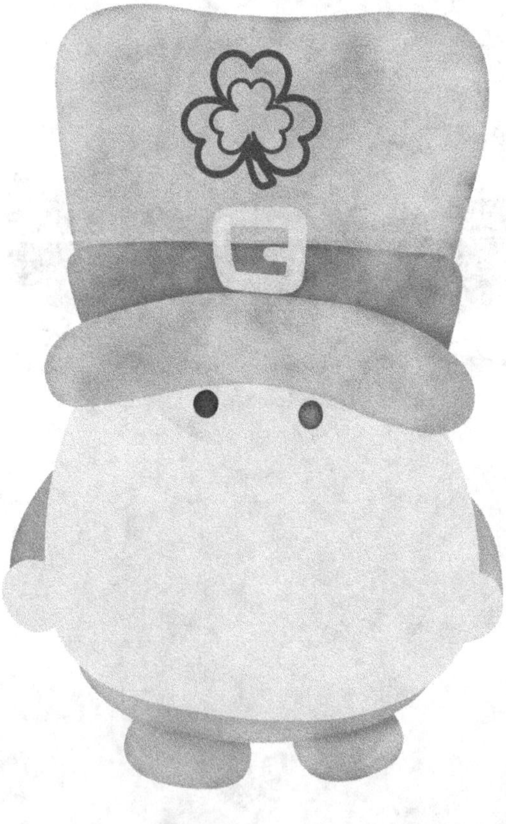

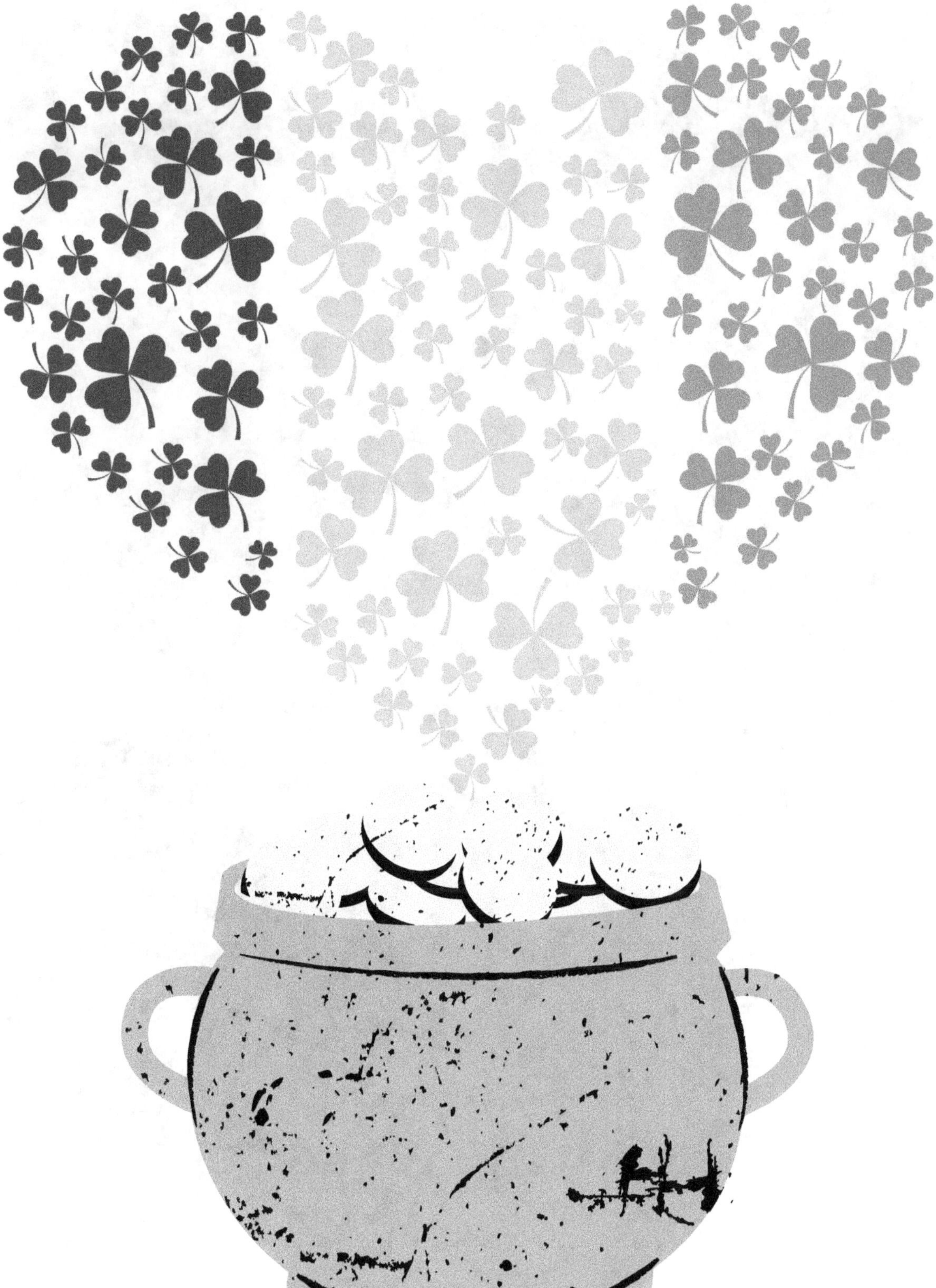

Luck
OF THE
Irish

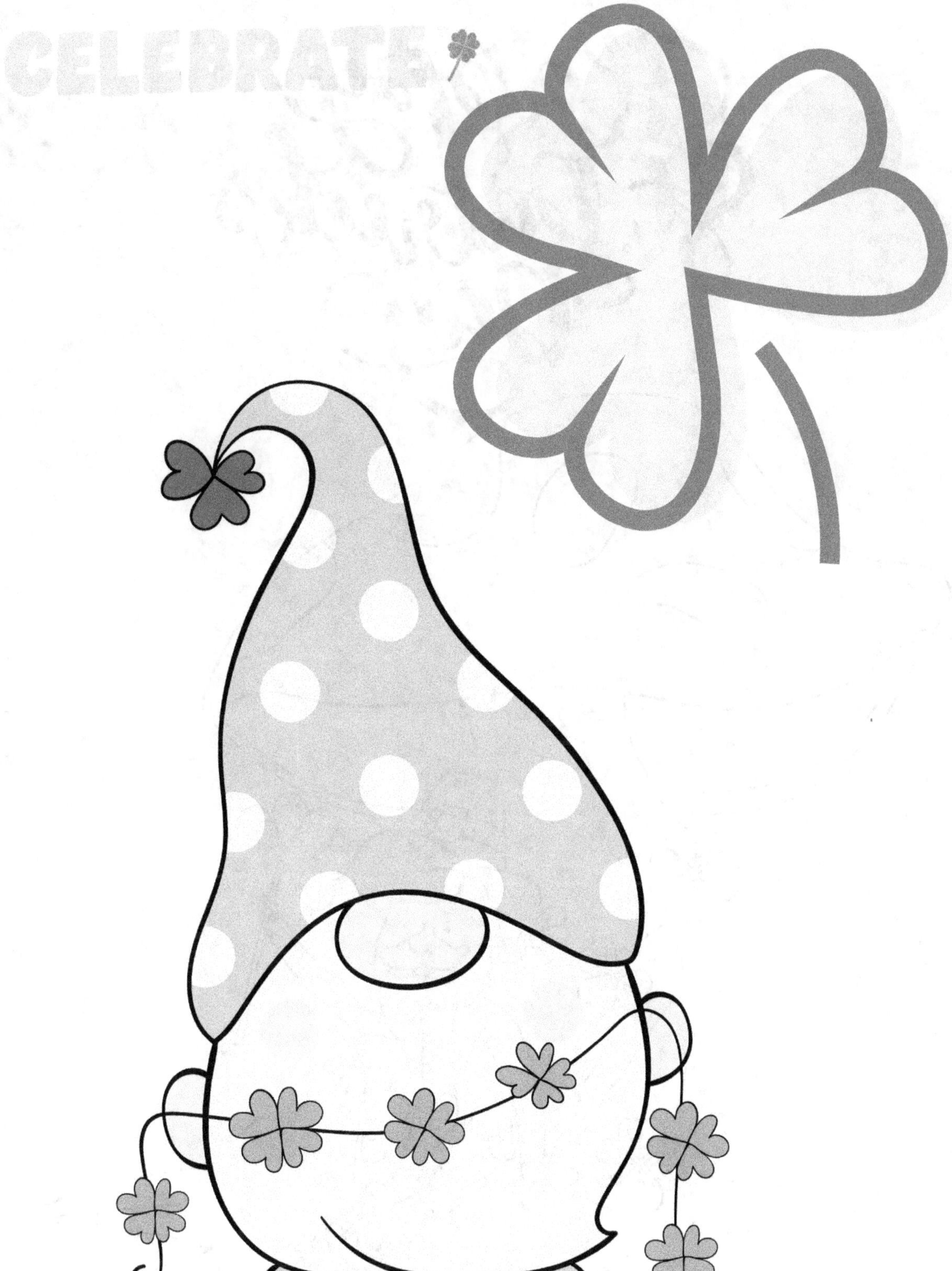
CELEBRATE

Happy St. Patrick's Day

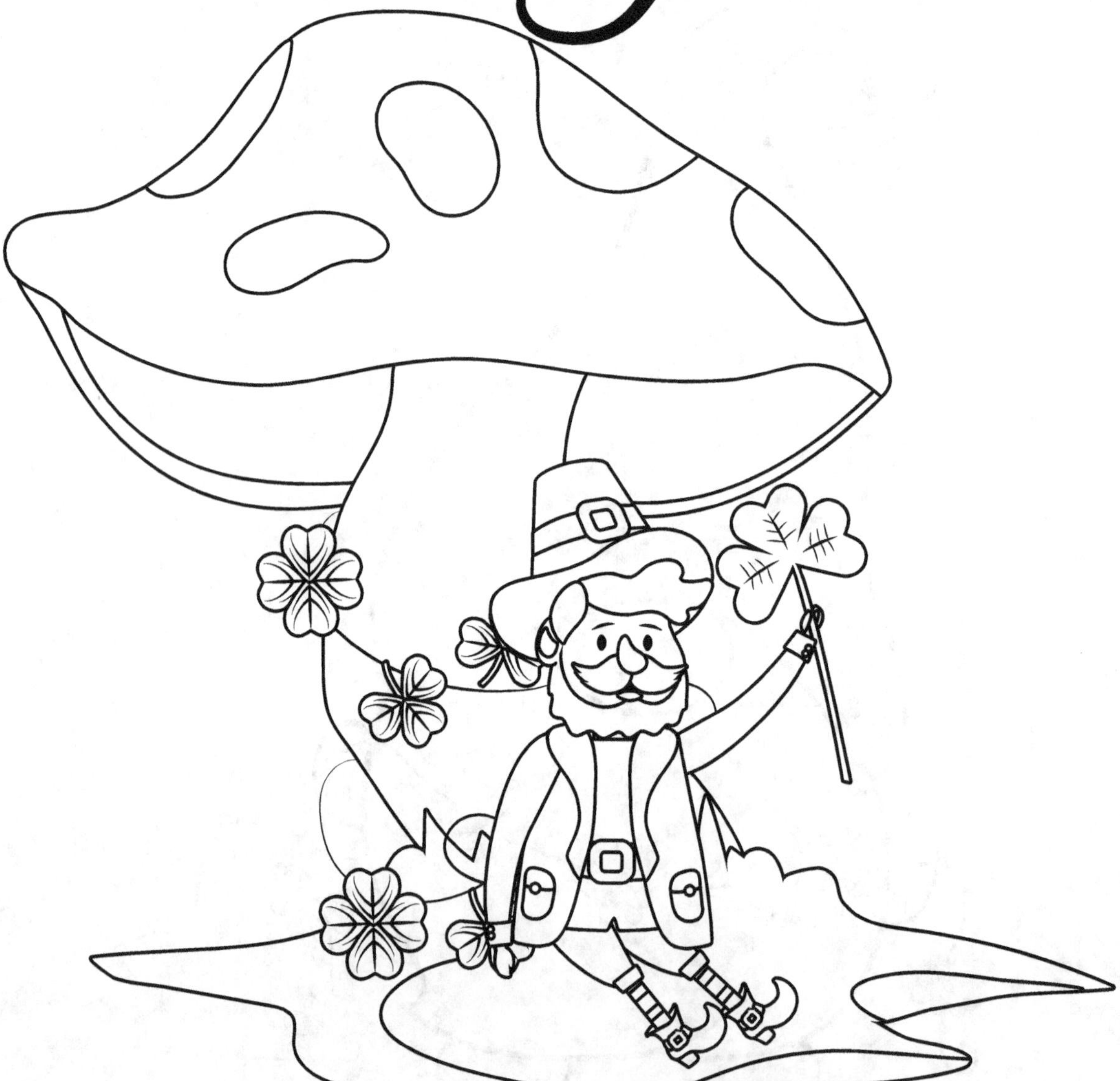

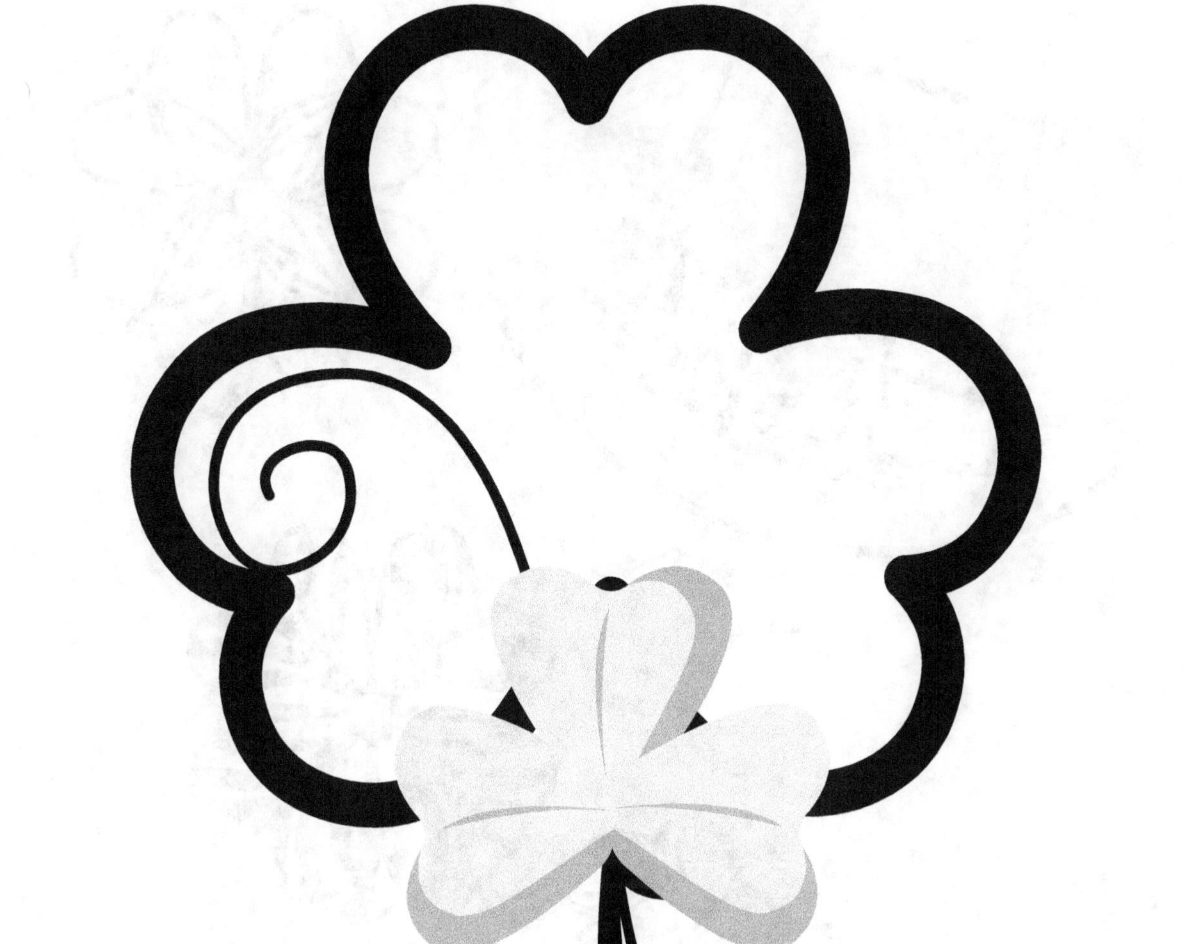

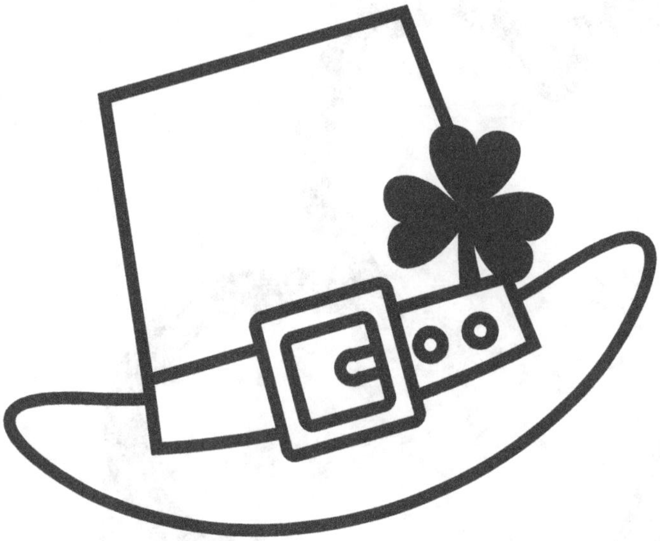

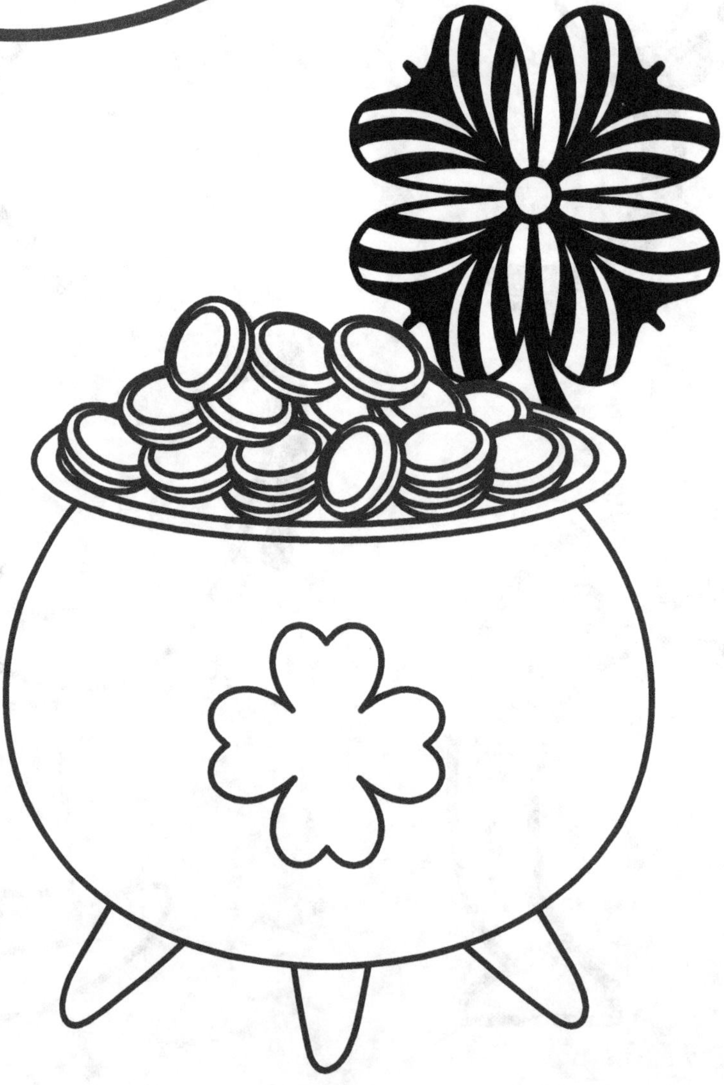

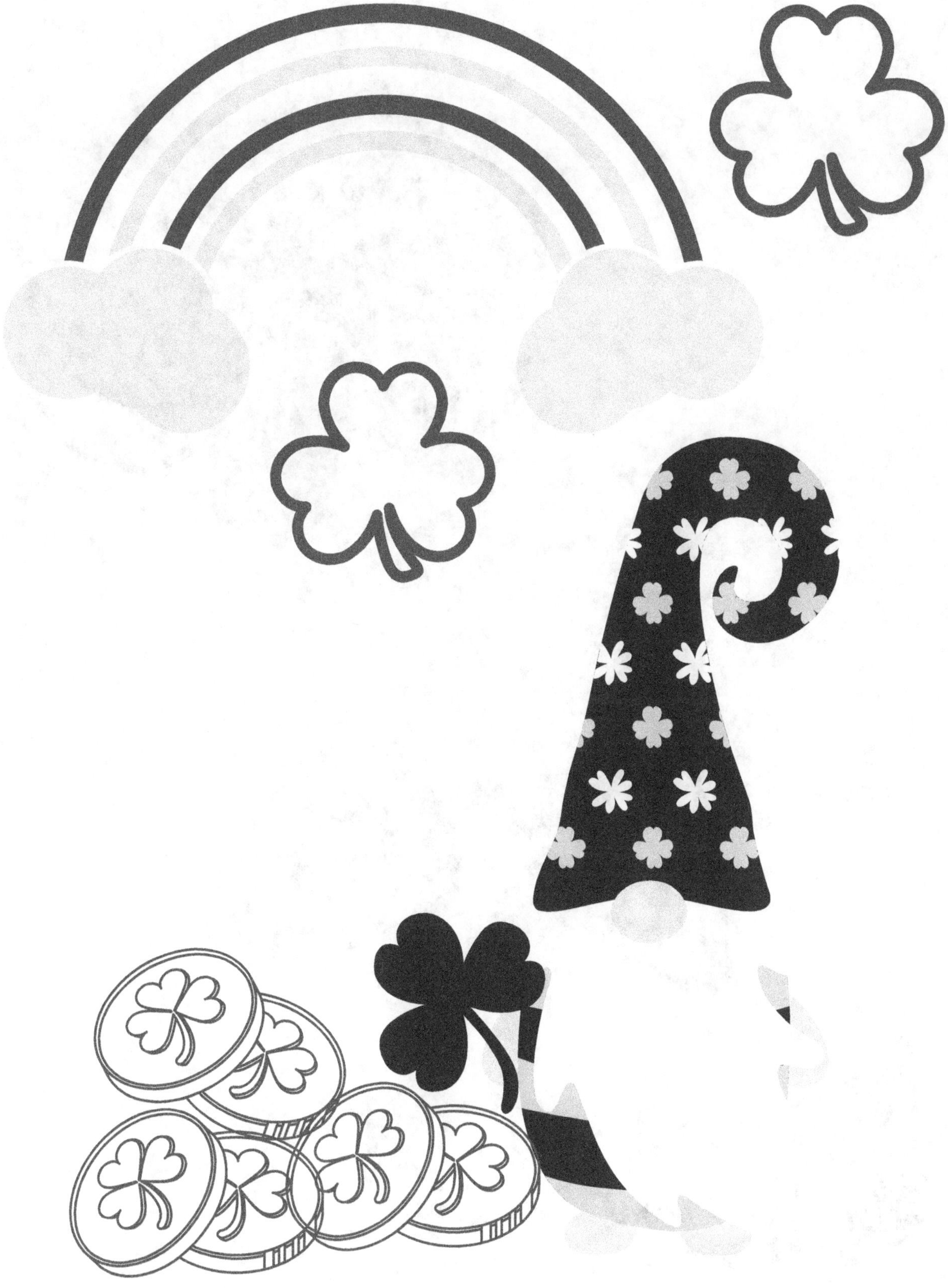

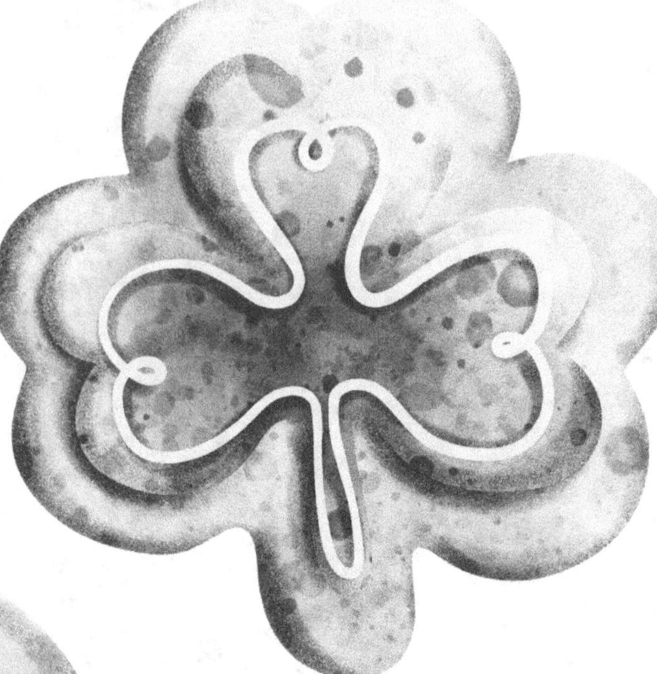

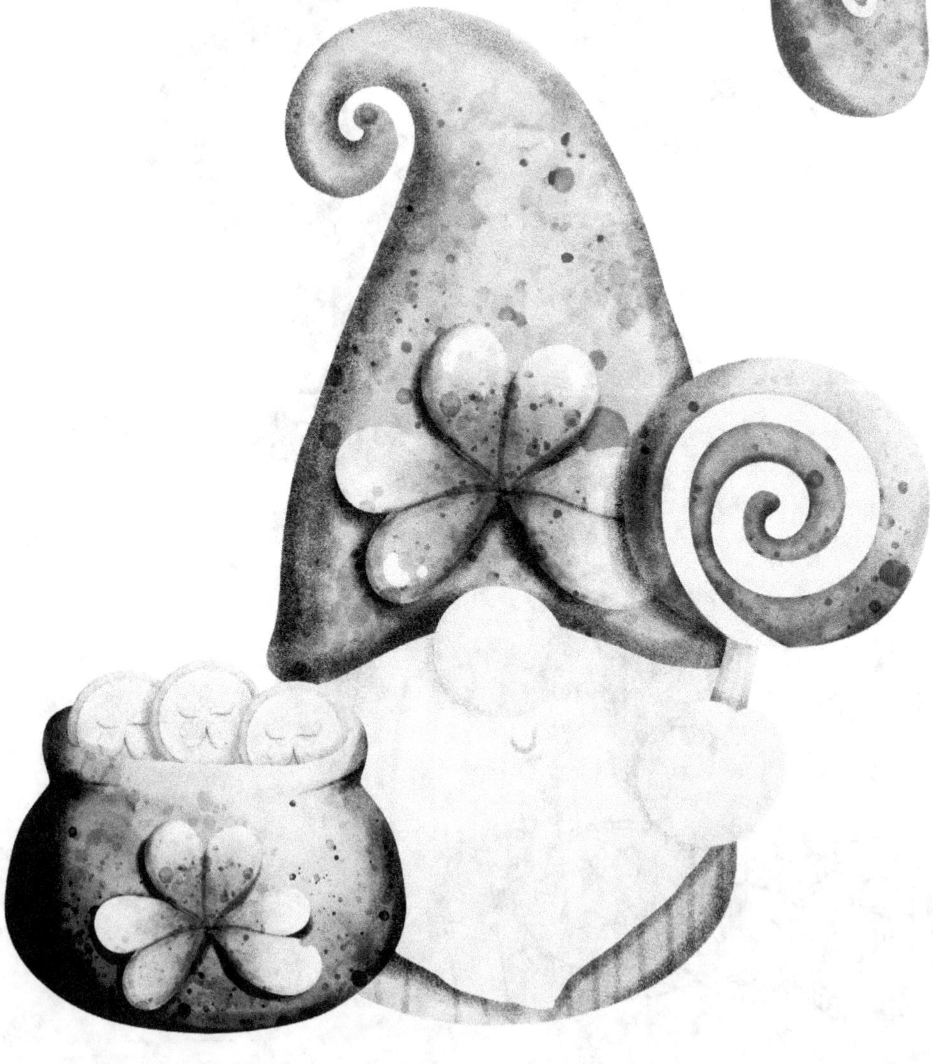

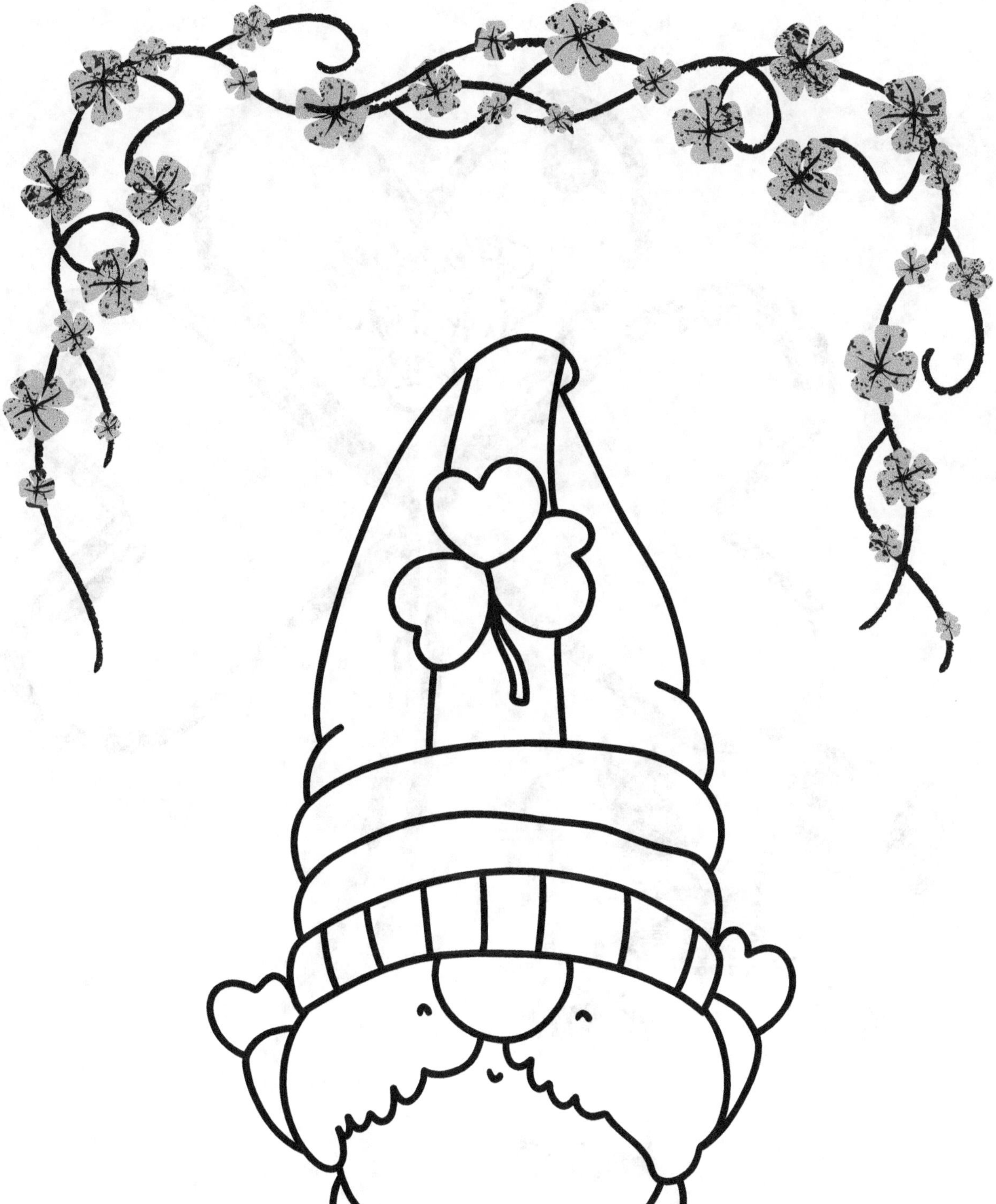

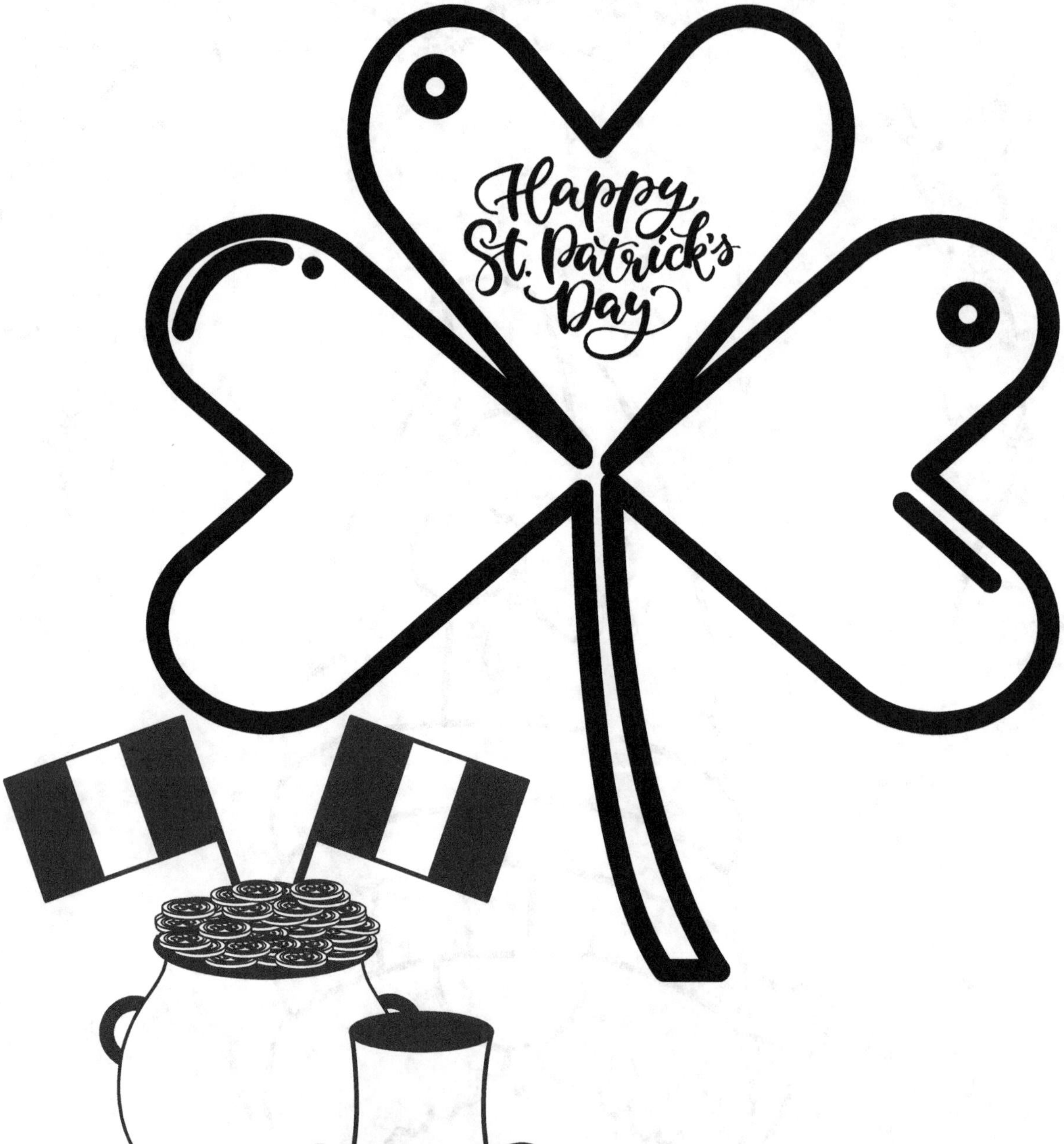
Happy St. Patrick's Day

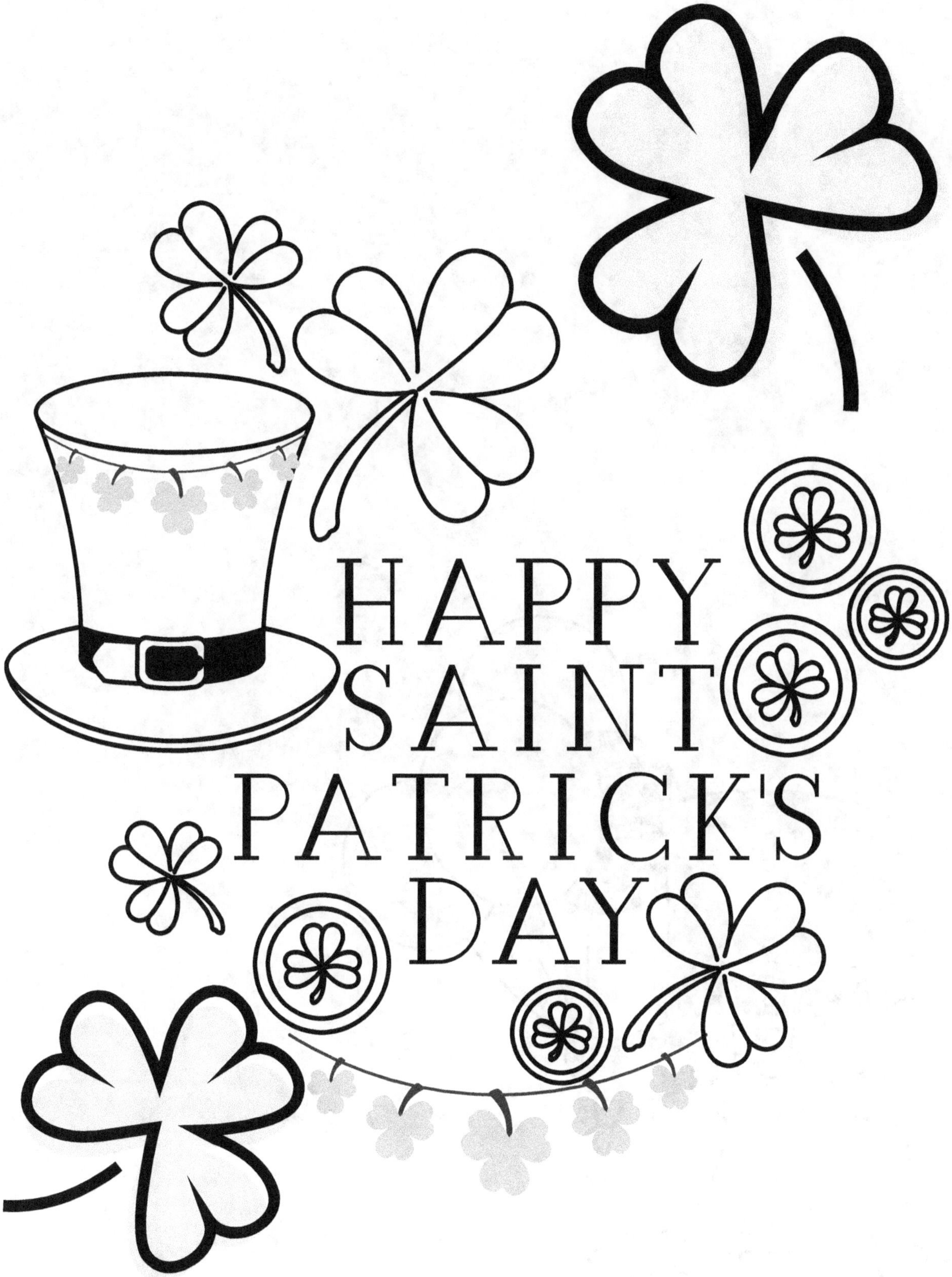
HAPPY SAINT PATRICK'S DAY

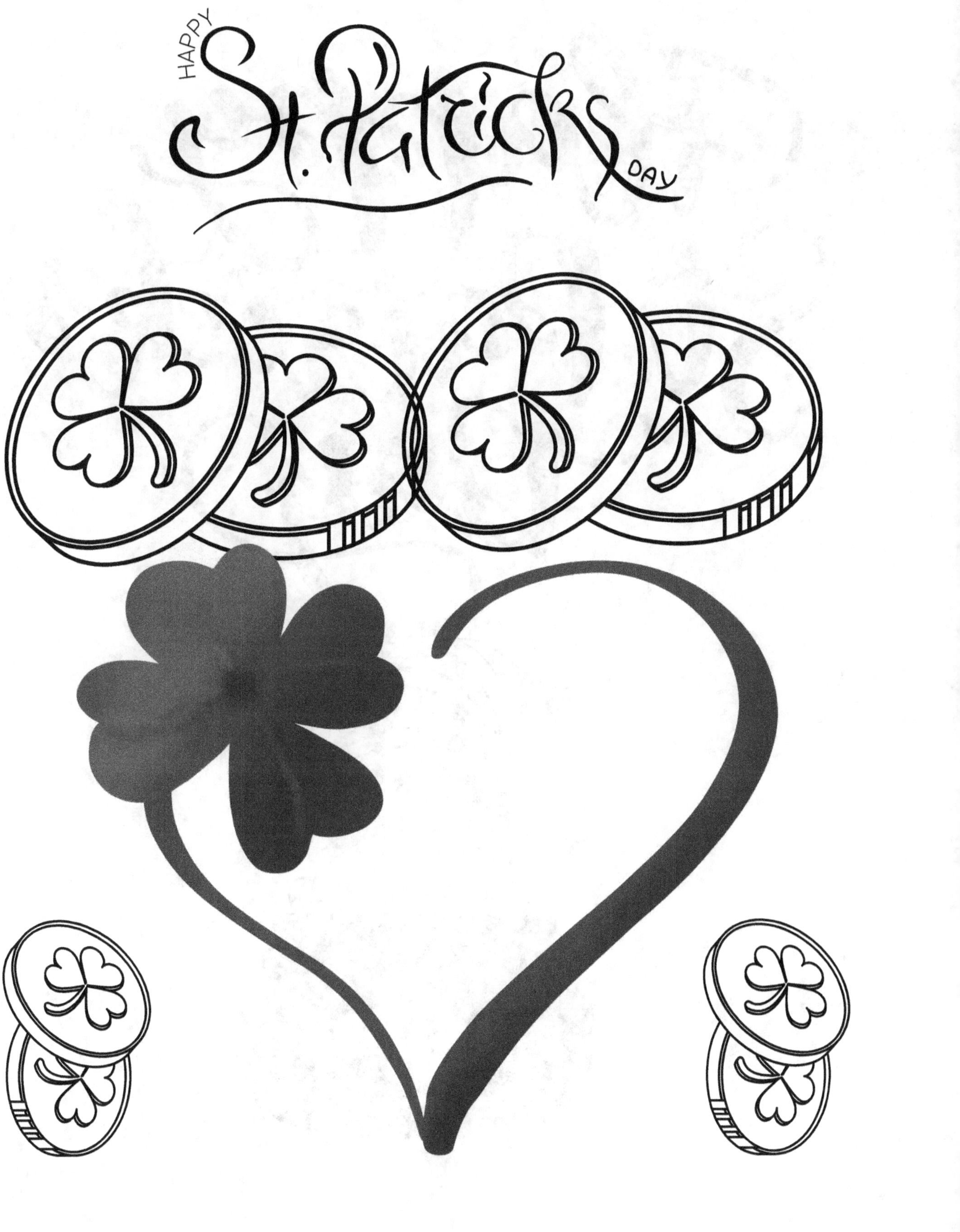
HAPPY
St. Patricks
DAY

Happy St. Patrick's Day

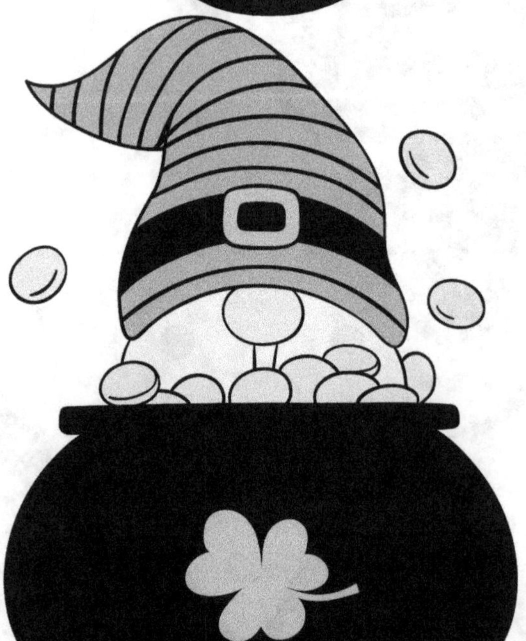

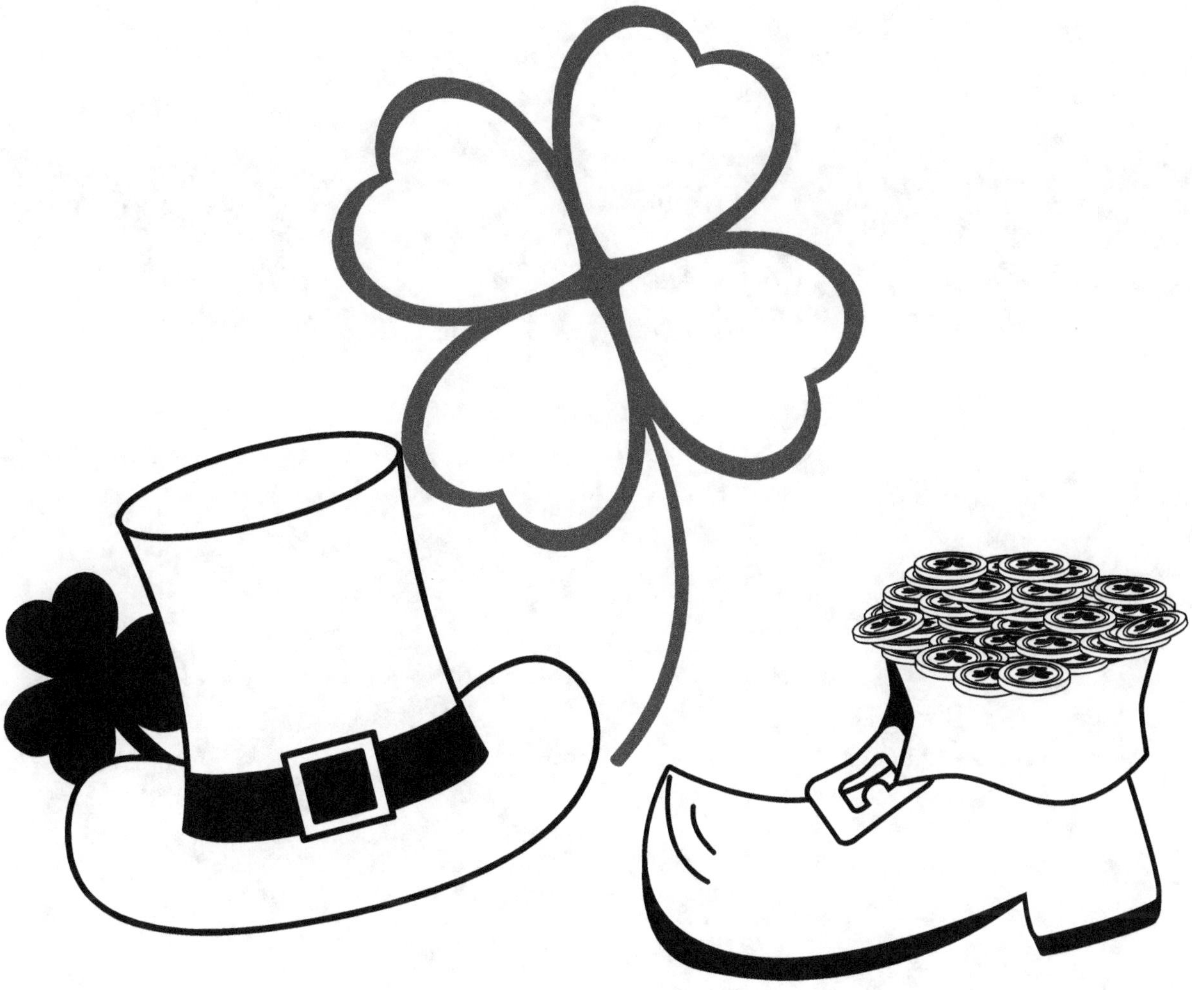

LUCKY CHARM

www.ingramcontent.com/pod-product-compliance
Lightning Source LLC
Chambersburg PA
CBHW080536220526
45465CB00015B/3367
9798376071526